A New Form of Government
T. Lee Burnham, Ph.D.

Dedication

To all those whose
Contributions
Have led to these thoughts.

When the war between the fledgling United States of America and England came to an end there was a great deal of confusion about where to go next. Soldiers were unhappy because they had won a war but had not been paid. They were planning a protest meeting to organize an effort to march on the Congress and demand to be paid and even take over the government. Washington found out about the meeting and chided them for even considering holding such a meeting without his approval. He invited them all to meet with him. When they were all gathered he took the podium and did something in public they had never seen him do before – he took out his glasses and put them in place in order to read his remarks. He told them that he had sacrificed much as well, including what was left of his eye sight. He was going to go to Congress to tender his resignation of his office and then go home to farm. He encouraged them all to do the same and leave it to Congress to sort it all out. What could they do.

The early attempt at governing (The Articles of Confederation) was seen by many as inadequate and thought was given about finding something better. Several of the founding fathers including Adams and Franklin spent serious time and effort in a study of past forms of government. Jefferson was too busy in France to spend any time with the topic.

Main among those who engaged in serious study was a very bright, energetic and perhaps a little arrogant James Madison. He devoted some serious time to a very detailed study of every form of government he could see in recorded history.

One place he looked very carefully was the history of Athens as one of the few examples of democracy he could find. "Democracy," in Greece was an attempt to create the "ideal" society and foster the truly happy individual. Pericles was seen by the people of Athens as a great leader in this effort. He was elected to his position of leadership in Athens over and over again. He wanted Athens to be strong and powerful and the people who lived there to be prosperous and happy. He carefully developed policies to win the world and gain an empire by commerce rather than by war. Since Athens was dependent upon imported food they built a powerful navy to guard the routes by which that food came. The people were wealthy, happy, well fed and proud of themselves. But as history soon proved – they were very short sighted. They were only interested in their own well being not that of others.

Cities subject to Athens provided funds for the defense of the trade routes against the Persians. Much of this money was used for the adornment of Athens (The Acropolis and the Parthenon). While liberty and democracy were the policy among the designated citizens of Athens, the rest of the Greek Confederacy was ruled by force as an empire of Athens. Jealousy and resistance to Athens existed everywhere. Sparta, Athens's old enemy, knew the strength of the Athenian fleet and contented themselves with supporting resistance and slowly forging a united front against Athenian power

Surrounded by enemies abroad and at home, Pericles worked for and talked about peace while he very carefully prepared for war. He stockpiled food and supplies. When war came, Pericles thought the answer was simple. He withdrew the population of the entire surrounding area (Attica) within the walls of Athens and waited for the navy to win the war. The Athenians thought this was a smart policy. The crowding of Athens, however, led to a plague, which raged for nearly three years, killing a fourth of the soldiers and a great number of the civilian population. The people blamed Pericles for this great calamity and they convicted him for misusing public funds. He was deposed from office and fined. But, when no one could be found to lead them they forgave him and recalled him to power. To show their esteem and sympathy for him they even overrode one of their own laws and bestowed citizenship upon his illegitimate son. Pericles had, however, been infected by the plague and he grew weak and died within a few months.

Under Pericles, Athens had reached her zenith, her golden age. But that success had been attained through the wealth of an unwilling empire and through the use of power that invited almost universal hostility. Does this have any parallel with our current definition of success – "win at all costs?" After Pericles there was no strong leader and Athenian democracy became almost mob rule. One leader after another did whatever they thought would placate the citizens and win their votes, regardless of the wisdom of the policy (public policy based on polls?). It has been said that the Athenian population was so used to having all the wealth and power it wanted that they became free of any moral scruples. They wanted continued prosperity and they wanted the rest of the world to pay for their empire. They elected whoever promised them the most luxury and comfort.

Finally, the unthinkable happened. Sparta, under the leadership of Lysander, sank or captured a large portion of the Athenian fleet. The Athenians were willing to do anything to preserve their power. They melted down the gold and silver from the statues on the Acropolis to pay for a new fleet. They gave freedom to slaves and citizenship to anyone who would fight for the city. The new armada successfully defeated the Spartan fleet and Athens thrilled with the news of victory. Their status was preserved. News was brought back that the crews of 25 of their ships, sunk by the enemy drowned in a storm. Hotheads insisted that the eight victorious generals (including the illegitimate son of Pericles recently honored with citizenship) should be put to death for their failure to save the entire fleet. This notion of "something terrible has happened, someone must pay for it" is the basis for how many public policy decisions and legal proceedings today? Socrates as a presiding officer of the assembly objected to such a plan but it was presented and passed over his protests. The sentence was carried out on the shocked generals who had expected a victor's welcome on the return. A few days later the Assembly repented and condemned to death those who had persuaded it to execute the generals.

Sparta was weak from the last battle and wanted peace and some kind of agreement between them but the Athenians would have none of it. Athens sent a newly reinforced fleet (with inept leaders after the execution of their best generals) to meet the Spartans thinking this would be the end of Sparta.   The battle was a complete failure for Athens. All but eight of the 208 Athenian ships were destroyed or taken. Sparta now took the upper hand and became absolute master of the Aegean. Athens was blockaded and within three months their stock of food was exhausted. Sparta demanded that the walls of Athens be destroyed. Athens had to agree to be subject to Sparta. Gone was their empire and their prosperity.

The empire that Athens had carefully built all around the Mediterranean was now destroyed and those who had been appointed by Athens to rule this empire were required to return to Athens. The new Athenian government was now led by those who had been forced to return home. They were an unhappy lot and not pleased at the lack of proper financial rewards for their leadership. They confiscated property, sold anything they could and either exiled or put to death any and all dissenters. They wanted to rule Athens the way Athens had ruled its empire. They put an end to freedom of teaching, assemblage, and speech. They forbade Socrates to continue his public discourses. The reaction to all of this created an eventual overthrow of the government and the establishment of a "new democracy." But the new democracy was looking for scapegoats for all of their troubles and they found one in Socrates. It was all his fault. He was convicted of corrupting public morals and put to death.

After his death, the Athenians regretted the decision and in turn put his accusers to death. Athens was exhausted. Gone were the dreams of wealth and empire.   Gone were the leaders who gained favor by encouraging efforts to placate the citizens and the struggles for power. The irony is that the new legacy of

Athens came from the teachings and students of Socrates. It was all they had left. They turned their energy to the study of philosophy and how to better the human condition.

Madison did not want to import the structure and failure of Athens to this new enterprise and discarded the notion of an Athenian Democracy in favor of the idea of a Republic where wise leadership was chosen by citizens of substance but not the entire public.

Madison also turned to the writings of Plato. Plato was very different from Socrates. He did not believe he could trust the answers he would get from asking questions and rejected the Socratic notion of seeking a "reality check." Plato wanted to know the best way to organize society and construct governmental systems. But every time he attempted to put his theories into actual practice they failed. He had no system of obtaining a reality check and testing his ideas because of his belief that human perception was faulty and could not be trusted. His position was that his best source of "truth" was his own internal logic. Basically he said: "If I think something it must be true simply because I think it." (NOTE: Does that sound at all familiar?)

Another school of thought visited by Madison was voiced by Charles Hobbs. Hobbs said that to think too much about your condition in life would bring unhappiness. Self-examination and introspection are unhealthy and unnecessary. Hobbs supported the notion of the "Devine Right of Kings to Rule," and said that individuals must simply accept the fact that your status in life is determined by your birth. Some are born to rule and others are born to be ruled. Life is very simple. Accept it. The birth of the English Republic under Cromwell was of great interest to Madison in this light. The English did a very unthinkable thing, that challenged Hobbs' principles. The English population executed one king and after a brief fling with a republic invited the son of the ruler they had executed to become their king. What gave the people the right to depose one ruler and then establish another?

Here on the scene came the teachings of John Locke. Madison was fascinated with the writings of John Locke at least in part because Locke was also the favorite of Thomas Jefferson. Locke said that the mind is a blank slate. Status is not determined by birth, every one begins life with equal potential. Individuals are basically good in nature, independent and of equal value. He taught that all power of government is derived from the individual and is subservient to the rights of the individual. He believed that by everyone working together for the common good, individuals stand the best chance to be happy. He placed a great deal of responsibility for individual as well as societal well being on the free thoughts and actions of each individual. It was up to individuals to think and reason in order to determine their course of action, including the type of government they would create. Jefferson effectively stated the basic principles of John Locke in the Declaration of Independence.

Madison spent time in an agonizing study of what he thought were all of the possibilities and as a result created what he called the "Virginia Plan." He was so certain that it was the one and only answer that he fully expected all who read it to be fully impressed and agree without any discussion or dissent. Madison was a powerful force in convincing the Congress to call for a Convention to revise and improve the Articles of Confederation with the full intent all along (although unspoken) to present his Virginia Plan to the Convention. He was not only convinced that his proposal would be accepted but also that this convention would have little influence on the eventual outcome without George Washington's presence. He asked, begged and pleaded with Washington to attend but was met consistently with the same answer: "No, I came home to farm and here I will stay for the rest of my days." When word was received by Washington of a great celebration in his honor being prepared in Philadelphia to mark his arrival to attend the Convention he felt he had no choice. Just how much of this was carefully contrived by Madison we will never know. But Washington did attend and was unanimously voted to chair the Convention.

Madison's major contributions to this effort were significant.   He got the process started. He got Washington there.   He presented the initial document that started the discussions. He insisted that he be allowed to record careful minutes of all of their discussions with the clear understanding that none of what he wrote would be published until after everyone who attended the Convention was dead.   All participants wanted to be free of public pressure and any tendency to pander to public opinion so that their efforts and their discussions would be free of anything other than their best thinking. I recommend the careful reading and study of Madison's notes of the Constitutional Convention to get a real flavor of the depth and conflict of these discussions.

They argued and almost came to blows all of that Summer with some even leaving the convention in a huff with personal invective. One Friday after all seemed to be said and done almost as a body they told Washington to return to Congress and ask them to get someone else to complete the task.   They were done. They were tired and they were not happy with the final product.   Washington convinced them to think on it over the weekend.   We have no record of Washington's activities over that weekend other than that he paid several visits to Benjamin Franklin and it was later suggested by Madison in a letter that Washington was very busy.

On Monday when they arrived Benjamin Franklin arrived late, too ill to walk on his own and too disabled to speak.   He had written a speech and asked that it be read.   Here is what he said:

"I confess that there are several parts of this constitution which I do not at present approve, but I am not sure I shall never approve them: For having lived long, I have experienced many instances of being obliged by better information, or fuller consideration, to change opinions even on important subjects, which I once thought right, but found to be otherwise. It is therefore that the older I grow, the more apt I am to doubt my own judgment, and to pay more respect to the judgment of others. Most men indeed as well as most sects in Religion, think themselves in possession of all truth, and that wherever others differ from them it is so far error. Though many private persons think almost as highly of their own infallibility as of that of their sect, few express it so naturally as a certain French lady, who in a dispute with her sister, said 'I don't know how it happens, Sister but I meet with no body but myself, that's always in the right.'

In these sentiments, Sir, I agree to this Constitution with all its faults. I doubt whether any other Convention we can obtain may be able to make a better Constitution. For when you assemble a number of men to have the advantage of their joint wisdom, you inevitably assemble with those men, all their prejudices, their passions, their errors of opinion, their local interests, and their selfish views. From such an assembly can a perfect production be expected? It therefore astonishes me, to find this system approaching so near to perfection as it does; and I think it will astonish our enemies, who are waiting with confidence to hear that our councils are confounded like those of the Builders of Babel; and that our States are on the point of separation, only to meet hereafter for the purpose of cutting one another's throats. Thus I consent, to this Constitution because I expect no better, and because I am not sure, that it is not the best. The opinions I have had of its errors, I sacrifice to the public good. I have never whispered a syllable of them abroad. Within these walls they were born, and here they shall die. I hope that we shall act heartily and unanimously in recommending this Constitution wherever our influence may extend, and turn our future thoughts and endeavors to the means of having it well administered.

I cannot help expressing a wish that every member of the Convention who may still have objections to it, would with me, on this occasion doubt a little of his own infallibility, and to make manifest our unanimity, put his name to this instrument."

The motion was called and approved "Done in Convention by the unanimous consent of the

States present the 17th of September 1787. In witness whereof we have hereunto subscribed our names."

At this point it might be interesting to make a comparison between the revolution in the United States and that in France.   The biggest difference - George Washington.   Washington did not want power. He could have become the new King of the new country but he didn't. He wisely chose two people whose influence were needed to invite opposing interests to be supportive of the new government – Alexander Hamilton and Thomas Jefferson.   It has been said that Washington spent a great deal of his time keeping Jefferson and Hamilton from killing each other.   Hamilton wanted a Federal Government with strong central power in almost every aspect of life similar to the old Royal Government of England prior to the English Revolution.   Jefferson had quite another view and they were not at all reticent to strongly voice their opinions publicly and in articles written under a pseudonym blasting each other and impugning each other's motives. In France there was a constant grab and struggle for power ending up not in a republic but in an Empire presided over by Napoleon as the Emperor.   For a clearer understanding of this difference I recommend two books: *His Excellency: George Washington* and *Citizens: A Chronicle of the French Revolution.*

Hamilton believed that the national government should take a primary role in having a very detailed control over the economy of the country and proposed a National Bank. He did not get very far with his efforts (at least partly due to Jefferson's objections) but the final result of his efforts was the current Federal Reserve Bank which has influence over the banking system but is not (or was not intended to be) in complete control over all banks and all banking activities. For a modern discussion of governmental use of financial power I would suggest reading: *FDR's FOLLY: How Roosevelt and His New Deal Prolonged the Great Depression.*

Over the years there was continued discussion over how to handle financial and commercial activities. There was Adam Smith who believed in complete free and unfettered financial competition and capitalism with little or no governmental control of interference. Karl Marx, had a different view. He looked at the world around him and saw poverty on the one side and wealth and power on the other side. He said that happiness is always destroyed by an emphasis on production to create profit and the obtaining of property. The notion of profit would always lead to the subservience of the individual. He believed that all of this could be changed if private ownership were abolished and production based on the needs of the community rather than the whims of individuals with power and the need to create profit. In order to bring this about it would be necessary to have a government with absolute power to wrest property and power away from the individuals who have it now and share it equally with everyone. Eventually, this would create a community where all shared everything in common and all would act for the common good. His thinking created a school of thought in direct opposition to that of both Adam Smith and John Locke. We have seen that this kind of philosophy created a human services profession, which could only teach individuals to accept their subservience to the group. The class warfare began by Marx continued in the writings of his followers.   Milovan Djilas (Vice President of Yugoslavia under Marshall Tito) saw major basic flaws in this approach.   His book "the New Class," maintains that to follow Marx only changed the groups that had power and that did not have power but would never lead to a "classless society." This kind of independent thinking caused his arrest and imprisonment.   It seems to be a tendency on the part of the followers of any aspect of Marxism/Socialism that only certain people have the intelligence to make decisions about what everyone else should do and opposing opinions need to be very carefully and even forcibly suppressed. This approach sounds more like a reversion to the "Devine Right of Kings," kind of thinking.   Only certain people know the truth and those people have not only the right but the responsibility to tell everyone else what is "best" for them. This is perhaps best discussed in two books: *Lenin, Stalin, and Hitler: The Age of Social Catastrophe* , and *Liberal Fascism.*

Adam Smith certainly was not totally right but there are also some very serious flaws in Marx and those who followed him.   Pope John Paul ii grew up in a Marxist society and had some very strong opinions that he expressed openly. He joined with President Ronald Reagan to work toward the defeat of the Soviet Union. In one of his many blogs he said:

"The role of the State is always a hot topic and often comes up in discussions I have with others or in the articles, blogs, etc. that I read.

Many or most people seem to know/believe that socialism is bad. Yet the reason they give is almost invariably that the Soviet experience went very very poorly and that the U.S. experience was clearly much better.

This seems to be de facto evidence of socialism's inability to be a system of organization and of capitalisms triumph.

In my studies of both economics and Catholic Social Teaching, I have found that many people don't really know why the Church rejects socialism and they also seem to think that welfare or gov't intervention in the economy of any kind is 'socialist'. Some think that Karl Marx gets a bad name for the 'experiment' played out in Russia. That 'Marxism' wasn't what Marx had in mind, that in fact, he really just wanted freedom for the workers from their employers. He wanted better working conditions, choices, and wages for the workers--he wanted them to stop being exploited. Marx did believe that Capitalism would eventually end in Socialism because of its own contradictory nature--accumulation leading to the immiseration of the working class. That said, he was, I believe, misguided."

Marx's statements as described by Pope John Paul certainly sound very positive and something to be of value and worthy of pursuit. Who can argue against "better working conditions, choices and wages for workers" or to "stop exploitation." However the real issue may be in looking deeper into what Pope John Paul referred to as being "misguided."

The Pope chided Catholic Priests who in what he called their misguided zeal to "fight" for the common people found themselves involved as social activists fighting for social justice and income distribution. When you stop and step back to look at the implications of this well intentioned approach it seems very clear that the end result has to be to create an all-inclusive government with the power and ability to determine in almost every aspect of life what is in the best interest of each and every individual as determine by powerful, wise and well-intentioned leaders – leaving little or no room for open discussion or dissenting opinions.

Is this really what we want?

It seems to me that history is on the side of the kind of Capitalism that has created a strong vibrant economy in the United States of America with governmental guidance and restraint to some extent to create an even playing field and to provide at least some sort of "safety net" for individuals in serious trouble. But other than that to get out of the way and let individuals use their own what Ronald Reagan called "rugged individualism," to maintain a vibrant economy that has the ability to meet the needs and requirements of all without coercion and without reverting to the notion of central planning in all aspects of life which has NEVER been successful.

The decisions we make today will have an influence on the world we create tomorrow. As an example you might find "Paris 1919: Six Months That Changed The World," very interesting reading now that we have some perspective on how the ending of World War I almost set up for certain the occurrence of World War II.

Remember Benjamin Franklin and don't get stuck in your own Ontological Arrogance and Deficit Model Thinking in that you really believe that you are the source of all truth and that anyone or anything different from you is not just different but clearly deficient.

References:

Churchill, W.S., (1958), *A History of the English Speaking Peoples* (4 volumes)

Durrant, A. & W., (1932), *The Story of Civilization,* (11 volumes)

Ellis, J.J., (2004), *His Excellency: George Washington*

Gellately, R., (2007), *Lenin, Stalin, and Hitler: The Age of Social Catastrophe*

Goldberg, J., (2008), *Liberal Fascism*

Macmillan, M., (2001), *Paris 191: Six Months that Changed the World*

Madison, J., (1788), *Notes of Debates in the Federal Convention of 1787*

Powell, J., (2003), *FDR's FOLLY: How Roosevelt and His New Deal Prolonged the Great Depression*

Schama, S., (1989), *Citizens: A Chronicle of the French Revolution*

www.ingramcontent.com/pod-product-compliance
Lightning Source LLC
Chambersburg PA
CBHW070457290526
45791CB00005B/2146